WOULD YOU RATHER...

GAME BOOK

For Kids Ages 6-12

Fun, Silly, Challenging and
Hilarious Questions for
Kids, Teens and Adults

Jake Jokester

How to Play
~The Rules~

- You need at least 2 players to play.

- Choose who will go first. The first player chooses a question for the next player (player 2) to answer.

- Player 2 chooses one answer out of the 2 options

  You cannot answer "both" or neither".

  Optional rule: the answering player has to explain why they made the choice that they made.

- The player who answered the last question becomes the next asker. If there are more than 2 players, you can either pick any person to answer the next question or you can just ask the person next to you, going around in a circle.

Most important rule: Laugh, smile and have lots of fun!

Thanks for getting our book!

If you enjoy using it and it gives you lots of laughs and fun moments, we would appreciate your review on Amazon. Just head on over to this book's Amazon page and click "Write a customer review".

We read each and every one of them

Would You Rather...

magically create more time
for yourself

OR

magically create more money
for yourself?

live 100 years in the past

OR

live 100 years in the future?

Would You Rather...

be a ballerina

 OR

be a policewoman?

eat only burgers for
the rest of your life

 OR

eat only pizza for the
rest of your life?

have a motorcycle

 OR

have a bicycle?

be a warrior

 OR

be an emperor?

Would You Rather...

watch a win compilation

OR

watch a fail compilation?

meet your favorite celebrity

OR

be on a TV show?

only drink from a spoon

only eat with chopsticks?

be a president that no one likes

be a homeless person that
everybody loves?

Would You Rather...

be rich and miserable

be poor and happy?

see a circus performance

see a magic show?

Would You Rather...

be a man

be a woman?

have your crush date your best friend

have your crush date your enemy?

Would You Rather...

rewatch Harry Potter

 OR

rewatch Twilight?

walk on all fours

 OR

walk sideways like a crab?

have 5 brothers

OR

have 5 sisters?

live in a world with no problems

OR

live in a world where you can
be the world ruler?

Would You Rather...

be able to see ghosts

OR

be able to talk to the dead?

have a nice teacher that's
bad at teaching

OR

have a mean teacher that's
good at teaching?

have terrifying nightmares at night

OR

see things that aren't there
when you're awake?

go backpacking with friends

OR

go backpacking solo?

Would You Rather...

meet a superhero in real life

 OR

meet a cartoon character in real life?

go somewhere on a cruise

 OR

go somewhere with a plane?

be stuck in a broken ski lift for 3 days

OR

be stuck in a broken elevator for 3 days?

know the ending of every
movie before you watch it

OR

not be able to watch any movie
before it's been out for 1 year?

Would You Rather...

be able to speak and write
in every language

OR

be able to read and listen
in every language?

know it all

OR

have it all?

be a cute dog

be a lovely cat?

have blonde hair

have dark hair?

have milkshakes

 OR

have smoothies?

look like a toothless horse

 OR

look like a laughing cow?

have unlimited movies

have unlimited games?

have a pet mouse

have a pet rat?

live in a 5-star luxury prison

OR

be free but live in the poorest
country in the world?

mentally never age

OR

physically never age?

Would You Rather...

use your mind to listen to music anytime

 OR

watch your dreams on the television?

live in a magical Harry Potter world

 OR

be very famous and wealthy
in the current world?

Would You Rather...

choose fame

 OR

choose wealth?

be half your height

 OR

be double your weight?

look young when you grow old

OR

have the ability to become
invisible whenever you want?

live next to the ocean

OR

live next to the mountains?

Would You Rather...

always take a shower in the morning

OR

always take a shower at night?

have four arms

OR

have a third eyeball?

go snorkeling

go camping?

bathe in milk

bathe in a chocolate drink?

Would You Rather...

live in a place surrounded by trees

 OR

live near the ocean?

have a ten-dollar bill

 OR

have a ten-dollar coin?

Would You Rather...

be the most popular in school

 OR

be the smartest in school?

live forever

 OR

have all the money in the world?

Would You Rather...

ride a bike

 OR

ride a scooter?

have a pig as a pet

 OR

have a monkey as a pet?

use only a controller for
every device you use

use only a keyboard and mouse
for every device you use?

have piercings

have tattoos?

have short hair

have long hair?

have super strength

have super speed?

have a pet dinosaur

OR

have a pet dragon?

be free from awkward moments

OR

be free from embarrassing moments?

Would You Rather...

be book-smart

 OR

be street-smart?

be able to play the piano

 OR

be able to play the guitar?

be examined by a male doctor

OR

be examined by a female doctor?

type faster than anyone

OR

speak faster than anyone?

Would You Rather...

play baseball

 OR

play basketball?

be able to write very fast

 OR

be able to read very fast?

Would You Rather...

have skin that's bulletproof

OR

be able to survive falls from any height?

know the whole truth about
everything in the universe

OR

let some things stay secret?

Would You Rather...

wear flip flops all the time

OR

wear rubber shoes all the time?

move to a different city

OR

move to a different country?

Would You Rather...

have an unlimited supply of pizza

OR

have an unlimited supply of ice cream?

not have to shower ever again

OR

not be able to see your
reflection ever again?

Would You Rather...

visit all the countries in the world

 OR

be very good at any musical instrument?

wear old clothes

 OR

wear old hairstyles?

Would You Rather...

have a 2-week long vacation

OR

have a free day every other day?

be unemployed but with lots of money

OR

be employed and satisfied with your job?

Would You Rather...

stand up when everyone is sitting down

 OR

sit down when everyone is standing up?

go back in time

 OR

travel into the future?

discover the entire Earth

discover space?

have no internet

have no cellphone?

Would You Rather...

be a thief

be a beggar?

go for a swim with a hungry shark

take a walk in the jungle
with a hungry lion?

talk to animals

know every language on the planet?

always say everything on your mind

not be able to speak again?

Would You Rather...

drink sour milk

OR

eat rotten eggs?

do a school project in a group

OR

do a school project by yourself?

be good at something you don't like

 OR

be bad at something you love?

live underground

 OR

live in a treehouse?

eat a whole onion

eat a whole lemon?

have a rewind button for your life

have a pause button for your life?

listen to an acoustic guitar

listen to an electric guitar?

have a huge dog

have a tiny dog?

Would You Rather...

eat meat

OR

eat vegetables?

watch a movie

OR

read a book?

be Dumbledore

 OR

be Gandalf?

have one arm and two legs

 OR

have two arms and one leg?

Would You Rather...

drive a police car

OR

drive an ambulance?

be a leader

OR

be a follower?

swim fast

OR

run fast?

have good food

OR

be in good company?

have more friends

OR

have more toys?

change your name to "No Name"

OR

change your name to "Yes Name"?

be weird and different

OR

be completely average?

give a bad gift

OR

give no gift at all?

Would You Rather...

be known as a famous leader

OR

be known as a famous inventor?

fly a kite

OR

go swing?

have 1 eye

have 2 noses?

be blind

be deaf?

Would You Rather...

play Super Smash Bros

play Mario Kart?

be a pilot

be a detective?

have x-ray vision

move objects without touching them?

stop pollution

stop human abuse?

Would You Rather...

eat 20 potatoes

OR

drink 2 liters of soft drinks?

be sick

OR

have a computer virus?

Would You Rather...

be a King/Prince

OR

be a Queen/Princess?

watch a movie without audio or subtitles

OR

listen to a movie without any visuals?

Would You Rather...

call Mom for help

OR

call Dad for help?

eat cake

OR

eat ice cream?

Would You Rather...

make 1 new law of your choice

 OR

get rid of a current law?

gain weight with no effort

 OR

lose weight with no effort?

Would You Rather...

have hot weather

have cold weather?

have cereal for breakfast

have toast for breakfast?

celebrate your birthday

OR

celebrate New Year's eve?

be the opposite gender for a day

OR

choose your age for a day?

Would You Rather...

eat broccoli ice cream

 OR

meat-flavored ice cream?

eat cookie dough

 OR

eat brownie batter?

have good parents

 OR

have rich parents?

have eyes that change their color

 OR

have hair that changes color?

Would You Rather...

be an ordinary person in a perfect world

OR

be an important person in a bad world?

have the ability to fly

OR

have the ability to read minds?

have an ordinary home in an
extraordinary place

have an extraordinary home
in an ordinary place?

be famous

be the best friend of someone famous?

listen to old music

 OR

listen to today's music?

be a babysitter

 OR

be a dog sitter?

watch a movie alone

OR

eat alone?

live on a sailboat

OR

live in a cabin in the woods?

Would You Rather...

have summer now

have winter now?

be kidnapped by terrorists

be abducted by aliens?

Would You Rather...

give up your computer

 OR

lose 2 good friendships?

use a magical potion

 OR

use enchanting dust?

be homeless

OR

be in prison?

be a Gryffindor in the
Harry Potter world

OR

be a Slytherin in the Harry
Potter world?

Would You Rather...

be a lawyer

OR

be a doctor?

have the abilitiy to become invisible
whenever you want

OR

have the ability to teleport?

Would You Rather...

eat a bowl of spaghetti
noodles without sauce

OR

eat spaghetti sauce without noodles?

give up the possibility to use
your computer forever

OR

give up the possibility to use
cellphone forever?

Would You Rather...

give up your computer

OR

give up your TV?

be in an 8 year old's body your whole life

OR

be in an 80 year old's body
your whole life?

Would You Rather...

do something bad for the greater good

OR

do something good and never
be recognized for it?

have a car

OR

have a motorcycle?

eat a worm

OR

eat a fly?

have a yacht

OR

have a jet?

Would You Rather...

make a phone call

 OR

send a text?

play outdoors

 OR

play indoors?

be a wizard

OR

be a ninja?

be stuck with people you really don't like

OR

be alone on an island?

Would You Rather...

have rain

 OR

have snow?

sneeze milk

 OR

fart popcorn?

have go on a sight-seeing vacation

OR

go on a relaxing trip?

have super strong arms

OR

have super strong legs?

Would You Rather...

eat sweet food

 OR

eat spicy food?

be a tree that can hear

 OR

be a bush that can see?

Would You Rather...

live on a beautiful island but alone

 OR

live in a polluted city with
your loved ones?

go left

 OR

go right?

Would You Rather...

be incredibly funny

be incredibly smart?

have nightmares every time
you sleep but be rich

have amazing dreams but be poor?

go on a trip with friends

OR

go on a trip with family?

live in a world where mermaids were real

OR

live in a world where unicorns were real?

Would You Rather...

make an imaginary thing become reality

 OR

make real things disappear
on your command?

use the internet 1 hour per week

 OR

use the internet unlimited but
with your eyes closed?

Would You Rather...

receive cash

OR

receive gifts?

be a famous celebrity

OR

be an unknown millionaire?

Would You Rather...

play American football

OR

play soccer?

start your own company

OR

start your own religion?

Would You Rather...

have your crush like you back

OR

always know who has a crush on you?

zoom in your vision

OR

amplify your hearing?

Would You Rather...

hide

seek?

drink sour milk

brush your teeth with soap?

Would You Rather...

have a black cat

have a white cat?

chase your career

pursue your dreams?

Would You Rather...

play all day

 OR

sleep all day?

have a PS5

 OR

have the latest Xbox?

Would You Rather...

ride a ship

ride a plane?

have a cookie

have a cupcake?

Would You Rather...

be a ninja

be a pirate?

be Superman

be Spiderman?

Would You Rather...

fight in a zombie apocalypse

 OR

fight in an alien invasion?

be a unicorn

 OR

be a mermaid?

Would You Rather...

create a new holiday

OR

create a new sport?

have a laptop

OR

have a desktop?

Would You Rather...

have a sandwich

have a burger?

play more hours per day
but fewer days

play fewer hours per day but more days?

Would You Rather...

always know if someone is lying

OR

be able to get away with lying?

mimic any form of dancing
just by watching it

OR

copy a person's singing voice
just by listening to it?

be able to speak all languages

be able to play all musical instruments?

be a wolf for the rest of your life

be an owl for the rest of your life?

Would You Rather...

be a baby penguin

be a baby monkey?

watch Star Trek

watch Star Wars?

Would You Rather...

live in a cave

live in a treehouse?

have a cold chocolate drink
for the rest of your life

have hot milk for the rest of your life?

Would You Rather...

be able to talk to dogs

 OR

be able to talk to cats?

be very good at math

 OR

be very good at sports?

Would You Rather...

eat a beetle

OR

be stung by a bee?

be good at singing

OR

be good at drawing?

Would You Rather...

compete on Hunger Games

 OR

compete on Tri-Wizard tournament?

get up early

 OR

stay up late every night?

go to school whenever you want

 OR

go to school every day and
be the top student?

go to the beach

 OR

go to the mountains?

Would You Rather...

have unlimited food for
the rest of your life

OR

have unlimited drinks for
the rest of your life?

go deaf in one ear

OR

go blind in one eye?

be a robot

OR

be a cyborg?

be a wizard

OR

be a superhero?

Would You Rather...

have pancakes for breakfast everyday

have pizza for dinner every day?

have infinite knowledge

have infinite power?

Would You Rather...

live in a castle

 OR

live in a spaceship?

be fat

 OR

be extra skinny?

Would You Rather...

be an Olympic athlete

OR

be the President?

change the size of an object
without affecting its weight

OR

change the weight of an object
without affecting the size?

Would You Rather...

be rich and not be able to go outside

OR

be poor but live in a mansion?

sneeze uncontrollably

OR

fart uncontrollably?

Would You Rather...

ride a camel

 OR

ride a horse?

have a lion as a pet

 OR

have a tiger as a pet?

Would You Rather...

have sun all week

have rain all week long?

go outside for 10 hours

play Minecraft for 10 hours?

Would You Rather...

create a new holiday

OR

create a new language?

never take a bath

OR

never brush your teeth?

Would You Rather...

be able to control fire

be able to control water?

be 5 years older

be 5 years younger?

Would You Rather...

eat a grape

OR

eat a plum?

sing

OR

dance?

Would You Rather...

have no one show up to your birthday

OR

have no one show up to your funeral?

watch South Park

OR

watch Family Guy?

Would You Rather...

change yourself to someone else

OR

stay the same as you are?

do PC gaming

OR

do console gaming?

be the smartest person

OR

be the coolest person?

win the lottery

OR

be able to live for twice
as long as normal?

One last thing - we would love to hear your feedback about this book!

If you found this activity book fun and useful, we would be very grateful if you posted a short review on Amazon! Your support does make a difference and we read every review personally.

If you would like to leave a review, just head on over to this book's Amazon page and click "Write a customer review".

Thank you for your support!